His Woman

His Wife

My Man

By

Monica Mason

All inquiries should be addressed to:

Monica Mason
Simplymonica72@gmail.com
Face Book Monica Mason
Twitter: @simplymonica_72
IG: @simplymonica72
267-467-6866 (Contact for events, workshops,

My name is Monica Mason the real Monique Atwater; I want to first Thank you for allowing me to tell my story, my life. This book is about the trials and tribulations that I have gone through over the course of my life.

This book will be one of many more to come, however this is the start in some sense. It's a healing process for me. Because I feel as though my story needs to be told, it needs to be heard, because I don't want other women like myself to go through what I have gone through, the pain, the hurt, and the shame.

I'm pretty sure that there are many women who are out there who have gone through the very same thing that I have gone through but, scared to speak about it; because they are scared of what their family and friends may think of them once the story gets out.

But like I said, this is my story, this is my life. I do hope that in reading this that it will encourage my women followers to get the strength inside of them selves to find the courage to come forward and tell their story.

I want to thank everyone who has given me the strength and support in helping me deal with everything that I went through to be able to tell you my story.

I want to first and foremost give all praises to Allah (God) for giving me the strength to go on and to seek strength within myself…

I also want to thank all of my family and very close friends who stood by me and gave me moral support throughout my ordeal.

Thank you very much.

*M*o
   Monique Atwater

Dedication:

To all those who inspired this book, but
will never read it…

Progress is dancing to the same song, that
use to make you cry a thousand plus
tears…

Pain is the beginning of healing and the
end of what hurt you…

Table of Content

Prelude:

I'm tired God... I've been going through so much these past few years... Men treating me like.... Like a thing to possess for their pleasure.... I was just as bad, after my crazy situation with you know who... I still have trouble saying his name... he broke my heart, tried to ruin my business, and... almost ruined my mind.... I want to care less about caring so much for damaged and broken men... That was a problem for me. There have been times in my life when I've been lucky... and times when I have been truly blessed... I feel blessed... I'm flying high lately; Flying in such a way that it feels as though something greater than me is carrying me along... Keeping me afloat... a connection to something higher... Is that you God? Is that you? If it is... let me know... because, I've been swimming in this ocean called life... bleeding and doing my best to stay away from sharks... Sometimes the sharks got me, but now... I want to out smart the sharks...I want better. Let me know if what I'm feeling ... This good feeling... Is you God?

PHASE ONE

Welcome to Monique world

Its 2:30 in the morning, a male voice is speaking softly.... *'Mo, it's time for you to get up..*" A body stirs under the covers. The male voice speaks again, this time a little bit louder than before, *'Mo, it's time for you to get up..* The body under the covers stirs yet again...
The body under the covers moans as it starts to move a little bit more now...and the voice begins to speak *'Mo....'* then a voice breaks in… *'Damnit, I know it's time to get up James, shit, I heard you the first couple of times!!*"

'Well Mo-Mo, I just wanted to make sure that you're up, because you have a very busy day today.'

Mo then rises from under the covers and pulls the pillows back and lays it against the headboard of her bed as she positions herself to lay against the pillows. Mo scans the bedroom in her sleepy daze. Mo then begins to think about where she came from and where she's at now.
Her bedroom is huge. Bigger than any bedroom that has ever been made.

The reason why it's so huge is because she designed it herself. Monique bedroom itself is over 1500 sq. ft. That cost her over $75,000.00 alone; all her furnishing is well over 2 million dollars.

Her sheets from Boll & Branch. Everything in the bedroom is custom made for Monique Atwaters, even her bed. Her bed that is custom made for a Queen. Monique then looks at the other side of the bed where it lies empty. Even though her bed is custom made for a Queen, however there's no King to share her bed with. Monique then pulls her legs up closer to her chest and she begins to pout because she is alone in her own kingdom. A voice breaks the silence in the room.

'Mo, you're not moving.' Monique sighs and says out loud,

'Damnit James I KNOW THAT I'M NOT FUCKIN' MOVING, AIIGHT, DAYUM!' She says angrily. James speaks again, 'I was just wondering as to why you're not moving or wanting me to do anything for you Mo?' Monique then shakes her head and then says to the voice

'Because I haven't decided anything yet James, fuck!'

And in case you are wondering who this James is that is disturbing Monique. James is her voice automated Butler. Who does just about everything for her...he can do everything for her accept to be that man that she longs for.

'James, I'm sorry.'

'That's quite alright Mo, I do understand.'

'No James, you don't understand. You don't understand anything because you're not here; you're just not here.'

'But I am here Mo.'

' Uuugh, no you're not James, so just stop it please. Just please stop. (Mo sighs again) But there is something that you can do for me James.'

'Okay Mo, what would you like for me to do for you?'

'Well James, you can warm up the floor for me and turn on the shower to my regular temperature, you can do that for me.'

'Okay Mo, I can do that for you. Would you also like for me to light a path from the bed to the shower as well?'

'Yes, please.' As soon as she said that James obeyed. He then illuminated the floor from her bed to the bathroom where you can then hear the water running. Monique slowly places her feet on the nicely warm floor that James made happen. As she slowly begins on her walk to the bathroom...

'James...?'

'Yes Mo?'

'Why can't you be a real man?'

'I don't know how to answer that Mo.'

Monique did a half heartily laugh... *'Of course, you don't James, of course you don't...'* As she takes off her very revealing night gown, she then enters the shower. As the water starts to run down Monique's body; she starts to ponder about the neighborhood that she use to live in North Philly. One of the most dangerous neighborhoods in the City. North Philly.

While growing up there, Monique saw the worst of the worst. What she has seen while living there, you would not believe, yet and still, this young lady made it out. She kept her promise to herself. She left North Philly and moved to the Burbs, a high area just outside of the city. She made it out on her own and built a life for herself. She went from being that tomboy / hood-rat from the neighborhood to a world renown owner for a top-rated radio station in Philly.

Monique's shower is handmade, with its marble tile floors that is heated, the shower is made the same with tile flooring. The tile alone cost $25,000.00. Glass incase shower, showerheads surrounds the shower to where the jets from the shower head hits every part of her body. The main showerhead comes down from the ceiling to where it comes down like rain from the sky. She can control the shower with her voice with the help of James.

A voice breaks her train of thought, its James again. *'Mo, you're going to be late.'* reminding her that she has a schedule that she must keep. *'Okay James, okay, damn!'* Monique then steps out of the shower dries herself off with her nice expensive fluffy towel set. After she dries herself off; she then walks over to the counter were she sits down and puts on her makeup, everything is laid out in how she likes it. After putting on her makeup, she then goes through a door that leads to her closet, which is huge.

On one side of her closet, she has all the name brand clothing line. As she stands there trying to decide on which dress to wear

'umm, James?'

'Yes Mo.'

'Get the coffee going will you please?'

'Already done Mo.'

 'Ah, thank you James, you're the best!' As she stands there smiling holding up a Brioni dress. Yes, I think that this dress will go nicely for what I have planned for today as she says to herself.
Monique then slides into the dress that hugs her nice tightly framed body. She then walks over to the shoe collection… *'Umm, James?*

'Yes Mo?'

'Which shoes do you think that I should wear today?'

'With your selection of dress that you picked out Mo, I would suggest to you Gluseppe Zanotti.

'Ahh, great choice James, great choice.' She picks up the shoes and puts them into a slot in the wall of her closet she then presses a button, the shoes then disappear (woosh!). Monique then goes and stands in front of a mirror and looks at herself and says... *'Damn Gurl, you're fine as fuck if I do say so myself...'*

Then she smiles as she walks away from the mirror. She then stops in another room to where she has nothing but handbags hanging from the walls. Once there, she is now trying to decide on which handbags to choose from. Her eyes stops at tan and black and gold handbag, made by Balmain she then drapes it across her forearm and heads towards the kitchen which as she gets closer, she can smell the coffee brewing, she smiles widely, *'James'*

'Yes Mo?'

'You're simply the best at what you do.'
As she continues to smile.

'Thank you Mo. Shall I start up the car and switch myself over to the car?'

'Yes James, thank you.'

'My pleasure Mo.'

'Which car will you be driving today Mo?'

'Well James, I feel like driving the red Tesla Model 3 James.'

'Very good Mo, feeling sporty now Mo?'

'Yes, I am James, yes, I am...' as she then walks over to the foyer where there is a large Queen Ann table and two chairs that are made like a throne, she sits down on one of them. And there, she reaches into a panel that is in the wall and pulls out Gluseppe Zanotti shoes that James selected earlier.

She slides her nicely polished pedicure feet into them she then stands up and looks one last time at the mirror *'Shit gurl, you're fine as fuck...humph!'*

'So, Mo you're feeling better than how you were earlier?'

'Don't ruin it James...not now'

'Sorry Mo'

'Uh huh, well don't let the shit happen again James.' As she smiles; knowing that this is a daily routine with James and herself. So then Mo grabs her coffee and heads out to the side door which leads to her six-car garage where she hears the 2020 red Tesla model 3 running and James has the garage door open.

Monique then steps inside of her car, places the coffee in the coffee holder and then adjusts the rearview mirror so that she can see herself. She then says to herself! 'I just can't get ova how fine you are!'

James broke in and said, *'Yes you are Mo, yes you are.'*

'You can say that again James, you can say that again...'

'Yes, you are Mo, yes you are...'

'Uuugh James, that was a figure of speech...damn, you need to get with the program.' As Mo fix the mirror back to its normal position. Monique then pulls out of the garage and goes down her mile in a half driveway. With the power of her Tesla under her feet, with the power of the Tesla, she soon will be hitting I-95 south which takes her into the city.

Monique then cuts on the radio to listen to her station. The radio station that she made famous. There she hears her colleagues on the air. And they are doing their normal routine, going back and forth with each other about the BLM movement and all of the protest that is going on across the country.

Jaylen is her fellow colleague on the show, he is also a music producer and song writer and sometimes he will come on the air and host a show from time to time. He's 6'3 200 pds, solid. A gorgeous hunk of a black bald specimen.

As Monique listens in to the show, James breaks in 'Mo, as far as with your schedule for today, you have a meeting at 10 a.m. with the investors and the top Executives. And then at 12 noon, you have a meeting with your financial advisor...Mo stops James before he could finish with her agenda for today... 'Wait James, hold on.' She then turns up the volume on the radio as she tries to listen to what is being said. Jaylen is mentioning something about the show that is going on today with Monique...

'Yes, yes, we're waiting on our Gurl Mo-Mo to come in, she has an important interview this morning with some of the top leaders from the BLM movement and the Mayor and with the Governor of the state...but as usual ugh, we're sitting here waiting on my gurl Mo-Mo to get in and take her throne.

So since she IS the boss, we have to wait on her...' Monique shakes her head and says *'No dat fuccker didn't just call me out on da air, I'm gonna get his ass for this when I get there.'*

There's really no problem with what time Monique comes into the station, because she basically runs and have full control of the operation and the show. Because the top Executives are okay with how she runs the station, just as long as she continues to make them money.

Monique understands the game, she learned from the absolute best from North Philly. She plays the same game right along with them, because with her, it's the same thing with them, she's all about making that paper.

The Tesla races down South 95 leading into the city. She then takes the exit that goes into downtown Philly. She takes a left and roars down the street, she is about four blocks away from the station

. Monique starts to smile as she gets closer to the station, because there is a security guard at the gate. They go at each other every time that they see each other.

He's about 75 yrs old and man, he's a trip. And every time that Monique comes into work, he hits on her.

Yep, there he is, as usual, leaning out of guard booth, smiling as he hears the car approaches the station. Monique starts cracking up because she knows what's up. As she pulls into the entrance to the parking lot Monique rolls down the window so that she can speak to him.

'Hmm, Good morning Ms. Monique, damn you're looking good this morning...'

Monique giggles slightly because they go through this every single morning that he is working... *'Morning Buddy, how you are doing this fine morning?'*

'Well sweet thang, I'll be doing hella good if I woke up each morning beside your beautiful ass

Mo...' (Buddy then smiles showing all of his brand new dentures with a crown on the side, like most of these old dudes wear them nowadays).

'You know something Buddy?'

'What's that Beautiful?'

'If you were to be in my bed, you wouldn't be able to do a damn thang anyway...' Monique then laughs out loudly. As she waits for Buddy to snap back at her with one of his jazzy come backs.

'You know something Mo, if I did get the opportunity to be in your bed, I would take these dentures out and tear your ass up, make you holla for Jesus...'

'Oh shit, I gotta go, you got me on that one Buddy...' Monique then throws up her hand waving bye to Buddy as she is cracking up at what the old man just said. She's looking back in her rearview mirror watching him as he's continuing to lean out the booth smiling at her as she drives away.

Monique then pulls into her very own personal parking space which is close by the door. No one parks in her place, the last person that parked in her place is now unemployed.

She then shuts off the car and checks herself in the mirror one last time to make sure that everything is in place. After messing around with Buddy and making her laugh so hard, she did not want her makeup to be ruined. '*Yeah*

Gurl, you still lookin good.' As she blows herself a kiss before she exits the car. Then she gets out of the car and reaches back in to grab her coffee and her handbag and before she could turn around good, boom, right there in her face was Mary Jane.

'*Monique, you're 5 minutes late...!*' *she screams.*

'*Whoa, hold up there sista, back up off me. You don't come at me like that!*' Mary Jane knew that when Monique takes that tone of voice, she needs to slow down and back up before she too, be in the unemployment line. '*Okay Monique,*

I'm sorry, just that you have to get everything prepped and ready for the big interview.'

'*Okay, that's better Mary Jane. But I got this, so stop your worrying.*' As they both start walking through the door that leads into the Radio station. Mary Jane continues talking as they walk together.

'Monique, do you want me to say a prayer before the meeting today?'

'Uumm, no Mary Jane, that's quite alright, we don't need no prayer right now, but thank you anyway.'

'Okay then Monique, I'm here if you should need me!' As Monique continues walking down the hallway waving back at Mary Jane.

Mary Jane Norton is one of a kind. What kind she is, that's the magical question. She's a bible thumping religious frantic. Just too bad that some of the quotes that she claims comes from the Bible is all wrong, but she has a heart as big as gold.

Monique heads to her executive suite, which is built like her home, its custom made for her and for her only. The only access into her suite is through James. As she approaches her office suite, she raises her arm to speak into her watch and informs James to open the door, which he does. When you enter her office, her office is pure white with a customized office desk made of special type of glass which cost her an estimated $12,000.00 easily

Which sets off to the side to where she can see outside so that she can see the beautiful city of Philly the city in which she loves so dearly.

As she makes her way to her desk, she puts down her handbag and she then sits down in her plush Bentley chair. She looks across her office and views her white loveseat and office chairs which is also made by Bentley. No one sits there holding any type of drinks or coffee. Because if they should spill anything on her furnishing, they will feel her wrath in a major way.

Even though Monique may be a smart businesswoman, however, please remember this; you can't take that for granted, she still has that street mentality. She will bust you upside of your head in a Philly heartbeat, North Philly that is.

Suddenly there's a knock at her door that interrupts her thought, she then turns to her laptop that sits on her desk and turns it on to see who is knocking at her door. Monique has tight security in and around her office that way to make sure that no one enters without her permission.

It's Dalvin Goode and Jaylen Reed. The crew from the radio station, coming for the conference before that big meeting with the leaders from BLM and the Mayor and some of the local Pastors and the Governor. She buzzed them in, and they all come in and go over towards the loveseat and office chairs and before they could sit down, Monique speaks…

'Woah, woah…hold the fuck up…!' They all stop in their tracks with a surprise look on their faces. And they all look at one another wondering what's the problem?

'Dalvin, I know that you're not coming into my office holding what I think is that coffee?' Dalvin stares at her in disbelief.
Dalvin answers nervously and somewhat surprised by Monique and answers; *'Umm, yeah it is Monique, duh…'*

'Duh, duh…listen dickhead, unless you got $20,000.00 tucked somewhere in those baggy ass pants of yours, I suggest that you take that back outside in the outta office somewhere and dump that shyt. Because there is no way in the hell that you're going
to be sitting on my furniture and over my plush Persian rug with that cup of coffee, no fuckin' way.'

By this time, the rest of them move away from him because they didn't want to feel the wraith of Monique, not when it comes down to stuff that she owns.

'But, Mo, if I do that, wouldn't I be considered late?'

'Yeah, and?!' With a stern look on her face…

'But you said that if we're ever late for a meeting, that you'll dock us G?'

'Well you shoulda thought about that shyt before you came steppn into my office with that cup of coffee. You know the dayum rules!'

'But Mo…' before he could say another word, Monique cuts him off. *'But Mo nothing take that shyt outside somewhere like I said damnit…!'*

Dalvin starts to mumble under his breath as he turns to walk back out of the office. *'Wait a minute, hold da fuck up, what are you saying, if you got something to say mutha fuccker, spit dat shyt out, don't hold that shyt in mutha fuccker, say it dayum it*!

Monique then slams her fist down on her desk and gets up and starts walking towards Dalvin and before Dalvin can say anything, Monique was right there in his face. Like, she was daring him to say something else.

Dalvin didn't say another word, he just turned and started walking away, so Monique cuts him off and got back in his face. *'Yeah, that's what I thought. Dalvin, don't let this shyt happened again or your ass will be out there on da street with that other limp dick mutha fuccker. You feel me?* As she whispers in his ear.

'Yeah Mo, I feel ya.' As he starts to walk out the office. Monique continues to stand there with her arms crossed as Dalvin exit the room. She then turns and looks at the rest of them and they all are kind of shying away, because they don't want any parts of Monique right now. Because they all know that when she's in this kind of mood, it's best to keep their mouth shut.

Monique then calms herself down before she continues with the meeting. *'Okay now then, is everything all set for the Community Leaders, Pastors and BLM, Mayor and also the Governor?'*

They all speak at the same time as they all try to refocus on the task at hand. Jaylen speaks first out of the group.

'Yea Mo, we're all gud wit dat peeps comn' in. We got everything all setup for you and the rest of us.'

'Okay Jay, thanks.'

'Fo sho, Mo fo sho' Then there comes a faint knock at the door. You can tell by Monique face; that she was getting frustrated again.

Mo then looks up and says; *'James, who is at the door?'*

'Well it appears to be young Dalvin Goode and Lady Mary Jane Norton.'

'Okay James, let them in.' Monique falls back in her chair and places her hand on the side of her face as Mary and Dalvin enters the office. Dalvin didn't even bother to look at Monique because he doesn't want to feel that type of embarrassment again. And Mary comes in and stands there looking at Monique.

'What is it Mary?'

'Just letting you know that the guest will be arriving soon Mo.'

'I know Mary, that's what I have James for, he reminds me of everything that is going on with my schedule. But thank you anyway. So, kay then, let's get ready for a great show. Lets give the audience what the investors are paying us to do.' Then everyone gets up and leave, and as they were leaving, Lisette enters and walks right up to Monique.

'What the hell is wrong with you!'

'Woah, woah, hold on there youngstas, who do you think you are?!'

'I know who I am, but the thing is, who da hell are you!?'

'First thing that you need to do young lady is, you need to step back and control that tone in your voice young lady, because you keep forgettn' who the parent is...so slow your roll...'

'But Mom listen, I came steppn' into the station and everyone is telling me how you're just going off on everyone, you know that shyt ain't right.'

31

Then James breaks in, because the tension that's in the room right now is extremely high between the two. *'Mo, it's time for the show to start.'*
Monique and Lisette just stand there looking at each other, no words are spoken, until Monique breaks the silence.
'Okay James, thank you.' *'You're quite welcome Mo.'*

'Okay Lisette listen, I have an especially important interview to do this morning, and after the show, we can have a sit down and discuss this again

.' Monique then starts to gather up her papers for the interview. As Monique walks pass Lisette to head out the door towards the studio.

'Okay, but trust me Ma, this shyt ain't ova Mother.' (As Lisette said sarcastically) Monique then stops in her tracks pauses for a second then turns and looks in her daughter's direction. She then walks up to her and gets in Lisette face.

'This shyt as you call it, it's ova when I say it's ova. Don't you eva forget who's the parent and who's the child in this mutha fucckn relationship. So, let's get that shyt straight first!'

Monique then turns and walks towards the door again and then Lisette stops Monique in her tracks by making one little statement.

'All of this shyt that is going on right now Mother, it's because of him, isn't it?'
Monique did not even bother to turn around and respond to that comment. She just continued walking right on out the door, leaving Lisette just standing there in bewilderment.

PHASE TWO

HIM

Everyone knows who **_Him_** is, they just dare not mentioned his name, at least not in front of Monique any way. Because they know if they ever mention **_"Him"_** or make any type of reference about **_Him_** that will be a bad career move, so no one ever mention **_" Him "_** in any kind of way.

The interview with the BLM Leaders and the Mayor and the city council board and the Governor was a huge success as it would be with Monique at the helm. She expects and demands perfection from her entire staff, because that's what the investors expect from her, since they are paying her, her high salary. And so, she expects the same thing from her staff at the radio station.

After the interview, the staff and Monique met back in her office to discuss the show. Which they do this normally. After each important show that they do, they all would come back to her office sit down to discuss what could have been done better, or what they should have said. Monique is always wanting to be better than what she was the day before, that's just her demand on herself, which is a lot of pressure for anyone, and she knows that.

Monique is sitting at her desk watching the staff talk amongst themselves, laughing and just having a good time. Monique then gets up and when they see her get up from her desk a hush fell among the room. Because Monique demands that type of respect.

Her light-skin 5ft 6inch tall frame, and her knock out ass body and her sexy dreamy bedroom eyes that would make any man drool over her. But like it was mentioned earlier, don't let this short frame businesswoman fool you into thinking that you can get over on her in the business world, because you would be dead wrong, she's always on point in that aspect Monique slowly walks over to the crew... and they all are silent, waiting for her to speak

. She stands there and pauses for a moment and then she says something that they didn't expect to hear from her.

'Listen, I know that I was a bitch earlier and I want to apologize for that, I am really and truly sorry for my behavior.' With her saying that, the looks on their faces, they all just stare at one another in shock before they could turn and look at Monique.

Jaylen gets up from the loveseat and says *'Mo, I know that I can speak for everyone in here so, it's all good Mo, we understand, that you're under a lot of pressure right now, you have all of these investors that you're dealing with and all of these other up and coming radio stations coming' at us and shyt tryn' to take our spot at being number one, so we git it Mo. So, we got you. Fo real'*

Tears starts welling up in her eyes, because she knows that they don't have to be putting up with her shit, they all could've just walked away when all of the shit hit the fan some years ago. But they didn't, they all stood by her and kept her head in the game.

'Aw that's so sweet Jay, thank you Boo.' She then walks over and gives him a hug. He hugs her back tightly almost passionately. And everyone that's there is starting to shed a little tear, because everyone that's sitting in that office has seen, and been involved with her struggle to make it where she is now.

'Well, I hate to break up this tender moment here, but Mo, do I still have to pay that G note for being late after you kicked my ass out? Dalvin said standing there scratching his nicely cut fade.

Everyone just bust out laughing and Monique then turns to and looks at Dalvin wiping tears from her eyes and said

'Hell yea, you brought coffee into my office space, you know da dayum rules...'

'Dayum, can't say that a nicca didn't try...' Everyone started laughing again. So, they all got up and came and stood in the floor and huddle around each other and then they placed their arms across each other shoulders.

Monique begins to speak.

Bow your heads everyone:

*"Dear father God, we come to you
again and beg you to forgive us and to
tell you thank you for Allowing us to
make it through this day together, in
Brotherhood, so thank you. And father
God, please While we are out here doing
your will that you protect Us from harm,
we ask you these things in your Holy
Spirit*

Dear Heavenly Father, Amen."

They all say Amen together and then
they all hug each other individually.

After which they all leave, and then
Monique goes over to her desk and starts
gathering up her things as she prepares to
go and do the business meeting with the
investors.

After gathering up all her things, she
heads out the door as she then holds up
her wristwatch and tells James to make
sure that her office is secure and that
there are no intruders are nowhere in her
office.

And of course, James complies with her demand. She makes her way to her car which has already been started by James, she steps inside and backs up and start heading towards the guard booth and you know who is still there waiting on her, Buddy.

She is already laughing before she even gets there. And as soon as Buddy hears her approaching, he starts grinning from ear to ear. Mo rolls down her window because she knows what's coming next.

'Leaving kinda early today aren't you Mo?'

Yeah Buddy, I got a meeting today with the investors, so I gotta show my ass there.

'Oh Baby, what an ass it is Mo, what an ass it is...' As he said laughing his ass off. Mo even had to laugh off that one.

'Buddy, you're sumthing else, let me outta here...' she said still laughing. Buddy then raise the security arm and said, *'Be good Mo...*

'Always Buddy, always' as she then turns left flickering her hand out the window as she roars off. Mo then puts on some music to help ease her nerves from today's earlier events and as she starts to get into her groove with the music, James all of sudden interrupts.

'Mo.'

'Uuugh! What is it now James, what da fuck is it,

You're interrupting my me time before I meet with these tight ass investors.'

'My apologies Mo, but you have a visitor waiting at the gate of your home.'

Mo then slows down and pulls over to the side of the street. Scared to ask the next question, fearing on who it may be. *'Who, who is it James?'* Shakenly scared.

'It's your daughter Lisette.' After hearing who it was waiting at her home, Mo then gave a sigh of relief and began to breathe again.

'James.'

'Yes Mo?'

'Pull up the camera feed and the intercom.'

'Okay Mo. It's on.'

'Lisette, wha da fuck do you want?'
Sounding all frustrated because she already know in how this conversation is going to go.

'Ma, tell James to let me in.'

'Now why in da hell would I want to do that?'

'Because we gotta finish our conversation from earlier.'

'Hmm, no we don't. As far as I'm concerned, that conversation has been address and undress and put to bed.'

'No Ma, it hasn't. We need to get this <u>thing</u> that's between us outta da way and then we can put it to bed as you say.'

'LOOK, that shyt has been put to bed a long time ago and that's where it's going to stay, and that's final!'

'But Ma....' And before she could finish her statement Mo cuts her off. ***'Ma nothing, the conversation is ova, now get the fuck away from my house!'***

Before Lisette could respond back, Mo orders James to shut it down in which he did

. Mo then peels off from the side of the road and races down the street towards the big IBM building in Downtown Philly.

She then pulls into the parking deck after she parks her car, she gets out and walks over towards the elevators and once inside of the elevator, she presses P for the penthouse which is on the 30th floor. When she reaches the top floor, she steps out and she's already in where the offices are. And once there she is greeted by one of the investors' secretary.

'Hello Ms. Atwater, the investors are waiting on you.' She said with a smile. ***'Thank you, you must be new here, I've never seen you here before?'***

'Yes, I am, just started working here a few days ago.'

43

'Oh okay, if you just started working here, how do you know me?

' That's one thing about Monique, she's always on top of her game and if anything seems suspicious, she is going to question it.

'Well Mr. Hillard described you to me.' She said nervously.

'Oh, really. So HOW did Mr. Hillard exactly described me?' By Monique making that statement which was unexpected and caught the young lady completely off guard, the young secretary started stuttering and nervous and at that time Mr. Hillard rapidly approached them both smiling awkwardly.

'Ah, Mo, glad that you're here, c'mon in, we're waiting on you. Come, come, let's not keep the others waiting.' As they start to walk off together Mo still looking back at the secretary and then looking at Hillard, wondering what was said about her?

They then turn a few corners and then they were at the big conference room, where it holds about 20 or more people.

But on this occasion, it's just four people Mo makes the fifth. They all are sitting down at one end of this huge table and Mo is sitting at the other end.

Mo then places her handbag on the table and sits down and crosses her legs and waits to hear what these white men has to say. Which she knows that it's all bullshit and that they are just blowing smoke up her ass, because all that they care about is making money. As long as Mo continues to make them money, they don't give a damn about anything else.

'Hello Mo, well we're glad that you showed up today for this meeting and to let you know that we heard the interview that you gave this morning and we couldn't be more prouder of you. The ratings went through the roof. We've been getting calls after calls to and from companies who want to endorse us well not us, but you and the radio station.

Mo sits there eyeing all of them sitting there with their fake ass smiles, knowing that they're trying to run game on her. But she has a trick for their asses in this meeting.

As she begins to speak with a slight smirk on her face, she gets up from the table and starts walking towards them, which is unusual for her to do that, because in the past meetings, Mo has always sat there quietly and took it all in, waiting for her time and her time is now.

'Hello Mr. Hillard and thank you for the information about companies wanting to endorse the radio station. As you very well know, that's my baby right there, so thank you.'

'You're quite welcome Mo. And it should be us thanking you, since you and Rashid....'
He then pauses and realizes that he made a huge mistake, a very BIG mistake. Saying his name in front of her.

The facial expression that Monique had on her face and the way that she stared at Hillard, I would not wish that on any human being alive or dead. So after hearing that name, she knew in what she was about to say was the right move for her. And she now knew what that young secretary was scared to say in front of her.

These mutha fucckers have been talking about me behind my back and now they're either wanting to squeeze me out or fuck me over some kind of way. But Monique put on a brave face, like the saying goes, I can show you betta than I can tell ya…She knows all to well in how to play the game, and she knows it far to well.

'Ah yes, Rashid and I did start this radio station together some years ago. And after getting together with you guys here, you paid me a lot of money to do what I do best, and I did that. Over the past year and a half or so, I brought you nothing but a profit. After which I was able to kick his ass to the curb, as we say from the Hood.

So, it should be me thanking you all for allowing me to do that, so that I can get my baby back where she belongs, with me…'

And before Mo could finish her statement, Hillard cut in and said *'Umm, you mean our Baby, don't you Mo?'*

Mo then walks over behind Mr. Hillard and places her arms around his shoulders and leans down and said in a soft voice in his ear…

'*No, I mean my Baby...I had her, I gave birth to her, so she's mines all mines.*' Hillard with a nervous giggle said... '*Wha, wha do you mean. We're business partners?*'

'*Nope, I'm afraid not gentlemen, as of 6 am this morning, wait, hold on lemme check on that, James, isn't that right?*' James spoke '*That is correct Mo.*'

'*So with that being said gentlemen, as of 6 am this morning, I own every inch, every crack which I am planning on getting that fixed by the way...*

I own 100 HOT FM .' Mo said confidently.

Hillard became really nervous and begun stuttering.... '*Wait, huh what, how could you...how, when!!!???*'

Mo started laughing proudly... '*Over time gentlemen, I brought you out, until it became final this morning. That secret corporation that you guys been in talks with about buying my baby, well that was me.*'

All of the men in the room became befuddled and shocked and stared at one another and wondered how this could happen? And before anyone could say another word Mo grabs her handbag and heads towards the door looking back at them and said, *'You guys fucked with the wrong bitch!'* She then threw two fingers and yelled out *DEUCES*...! And also her middle finger for good measure.

Then she walks by that new secretary and leaned down and whispered *'Honey, I am that nicca bitch that they told you about...'* she then leans back up and the look on that secretary was priceless and Mo then turns and walks out laughing her ass off.

Mo then jumps into her Tesla Model 3 and heads towards the exit and then when she hits the main street, she squeal the tires as she heads to her financial advisor. Thinking to herself, ***<u>dayum, it sure feels good being the fucker this time instead of the person being fucked</u>***...as she thought to herself with a wide smile on her face.

Within minutes Mo is in the Financial District of Downtown Philly. She pulls into the parking lot and shuts off the car and grabs her handbag and steps out the car, fixes her dress and goes into the financial building and get's on an elevator and presses the 3rd floor. Once there she heads to these two huge mahogany doors and there on the doors in huge black letters it reads **BLACK & BLACK** Mo can't stop from laughing. Every time that she goes and see her Financial Advisor,

she reads the name on the door, and she cracks up.

Once inside she is greeted by an African American female secretary. When she looks up and sees Mo, she then greets her with a smile… *'Hello there Mo, how you doing?*

'I'm good Trina, and how about you?'

'Gurl, I'm doing great…' When Mo heard her say that, both Mo and Trina laugh together. *'Is Tim in, I think that he's expecting me?'*

'Yes Mo, he's in there waiting on you and I can't wait to hear how it went with the investors.'

'Well gurl come on in and I'll tell you both what happened.' Trina then calls Tim Walton on the phone to let him know that Mo is here. Tim response was okay, send her in.

'Okay Mr. Walton, however, Mo wants me to come in as well, is that okay with you?'

'Yes, it is, since you were a part of this as well, so yeah, you can join us.' So, they both entered Tim Waltons' office. The gentleman behind the desk gets up and walks around his big black desk and greets Mo with a hug and kiss on the cheek.

'Well Mo, please have a seat and tell me how it went when you broke the news to them in how now you now own 100% of your baby 100 HOT FM?' As he goes back and sits down behind his desk.

Mo then sits down, and Trina pulls up a chair and sits down besides Mo. Mo then start telling them both in every detail in what happened at the investor meeting. Nodding his head and smiling at the same time, Tim is enjoying every bit of what is being said by Mo.

And after Mo finish telling them both about what happened, Mr. Walton begins talking; *'Told you Mo, I knew that they would try this shyt when you first came to me. I knew that these Mutha Fucckers was corrupt enough and stupid enough to want to get rid of you so that they could sale 100 FM to someone else and make a tidy little profit for themselves. They've always done that, so I know how these white fucckers roll.*

'Yes Tim, you did tell me, just that I was hoping that they would give me the opportunity to at least try to make some sort of arrangement with them or something for me to buy my station.'

'Nah, these crackers are greedy, they always have been greedy. No way possible were they gonna allow for some rich black woman to own anything.'

'I see that now, so thank you Tim, thank you so much for teaching me and showing me the books and where every penny of my money is going and how it is being used to make me more money.'

'Mo please stop, it was an honor in doing it. Glad that Trina and I could help you reach your goal and beyond that.'

'I am honored to have met you Tim, I am beyond words. I am profoundly grateful.'

'Mo, this is your season, this is your season to show the world who Monique Atwaters is.' Mo sits there with tears welling up in her eyes.'

'Nooo, we'll have none of that Mo, no crying in this dayum office...' Tim said with a smile on his face. Mo then smiles back at him trying to hold back the tears.

'So, what happens now Tim?'

'Well I did manage to get in touch with the companies that are willing to endorse you and I have everything recorded for you so that way you can hear the conversation that I had with them. Because as you know Mo, I believe in transparency. My clients have to be aware of what goes on here, they just have to.

So that way it won't cause any conflict like that I'm stealing from them or whatever the case. I want my people to know what we're doing here. So, like I said, I'll send you the recordings and as a matter of fact, I have your first endorsement check right here.'

Tim then reaches inside of his desk and pulls out a check and hands it over to Mo so that she can see it. And the look on Mo's face was a look of shock and disbelief.

'Oh my God Tim, you can't be serious.' As Mo said with a huge smile on her face. Tim smiles at her and says, *'Yes Mo, I am serious, you have the check right there in your hand.'*

'Oh my fucckn God Tim, I have neva in my life seen so many numbers and zeros all on one check!' Mo then jumps up and runs over to Tim and gives him a great big hug.

Tim is shocked and surprised by her reaction and hugs her back. *'Glad to help Mo, glad to help.'*

Mo then goes over and hugs Trina and Trina then hugs her back as well as they both stand there with tears in their eyes. Mo then looks back over her shoulder and sees Tim trying to hide that he was wiping away tears from his eyes.

'Hey, wait a minute there Tim, you said no cryn in your office and there you go...' As Mo and Trina start laughing at Tim.

'Fuck you Mo.' Said laughing.

'Hell, with this check that you just gave me, I just might let you.' As they all start laughing. Knowing that won't happen since Tim is gay. So, they all sat back down as Mo continues looking at the check that Tim handed over to her.

'Tim, dayum, I'm still in shock over this dayum check. And here is the funny thing about all of this. Here you are, an African American Man. (Tim looks at her funny when she said that) ahem, I mean an African American, and here you are sitting here in the White Financial District.

In a building that is owned by white people and on your office door you have Black & Black, when no one in your office is named Black. Where and how did you come up with that name?'

Tim starts laughing along with Trina. *'Well Mo, it's really quite simple. I want these people here to know who owns and runs this business. And that is "Black People". I was playing around with the name at first and then it finally stuck with me and so Bam. And I said, why not have it here, they come to our community and open up shop. So why the fuck not that we come into their neighborhood and open up shop?'*

'I hear ya. I'm just so proud of you Tim.'

'Well I'm happy for you Mo, glad to help.' So, I get my normal 5%, right?'

'You know what Tim, for what you have done for me and how you helped me throughout this process, take out 20%. Hell, I'm fucckn rich now, I can afford it. Everyone in the room started laughing again. And Tim agreed.

Mo then gets up and goes over and hugs Tim one more time and then hugs Trina and she grabs her handbag and heads out the door back to her car. Once inside of her car, Mo screams loudly as she pounds the steering wheel in excitement. She reaches inside her handbag and see's and get the check and on that check she sees written Five Hundred million dollars with more to come with endorsements. So, she then regains her composer and starts up the car and drives to her bank to deposit the check. After leaving the bank James breaks in *'Mo, Lisette is still waiting at the gate.'*

With him saying that, Mo comes back to reality. Back to the real world. Her world that she hates with a passion. It appears, that no matter how far she has come, her past still haunts her.

All because of some of the bad decisions that she made. Mo says nothing for a moment and then she says to James, *'Okay James, thank you.'*

'You're welcome Mo. Do you want me to let her in?'

'No James, just let her wait.' Mo is now somber. She puts the car in reverse and then in drive and she slowly drives out of the parking lot and started driving, nowhere, she's just driving. Before Mo realizes it, she is parked in front of a church.

She turns the car off and gets out and slowly goes inside. The church is somewhat empty, so she finds a seat in the middle of the church and sits down on a dirty dusty pew. She flops down and starts thinking about how all of this begun.

Dalvin, Jaylen, Mary Jane, Ne'a Temple, Katrina Middleton and then there is *"Him."* The name and the person who is never to be mentioned in her presence. Rashid. ***Rashid Temple***.

The one man who she ever loved. They started out as business partners and then Mo slipped and fell in love with him. Not knowing that he was married until it was too late. And let's not forget Lisette, how she became involved in all of this is still mind-blowing to her. With all of what Monique has done to try to forget about *"Him"* She just can't seem to escape him.

We all were tight at one point, or at least she thought that they were. She was happy, her and Rashid was business partners and lovers. Like the old saying goes, never mix business with pleasure. That's a deadly combination. But you have to live and learn.

Mo didn't realize that Rashid was married to Ne'a. And Ne'a didn't realize that Rashid was involved with Katrina as well. Rashid was a complete lady's man. He loved women and he was burning the candle at both ends. Rashid knew how much I loved him, but yet and still he played me.

Not only did he play me, he played Katrina and Ne'a his very own wife too. And I did not know that he was also involved with my very own daughter.

When Mo got to that point, she just fell back against the pew and sighed deeply in disgust. My very own flesh and blood. That BASTARD!!! Mo then realizes where she was and said loudly *'Oh God, please forgive me...'* And then Mo heard a voice that broke her train of thought... *'He will...he always does.'* The voice said.

Startled by the voice, Mo turns and looks to see who's talking to her. There two pews back she sees a man sitting there with a slight smile on his face… *'Huh, what. Did you say something.'* Mo says with a shy smile.

'God. He does. He always does forgive us for whatever we have done in our past.

Because He's just that way.' The man said.

'Oh, okay, thanks.' Mo is still in shock, because she didn't think that no one heard her when she said that.

'No problem, glad to help.' As the man was getting up fixing his suit coat as he prepares to leave.

Mo stares at him with a faint little smile as she watches him leave the church. *'Gurl, you gotta be more careful in what you say or where you're at.'* Mo then turns back around and starts back thinking again as she places her head in her hands. Trying to come back to reality. But she just can't escape it. She just can't. How can this man who I loved get involved with my very own daughter???

I just can't wrap my head around that.
And how dumb could I have been and not
seen any of this. She continues to think.

But I shoulda known something was up
when he would start blowing me off when
I had invited him over for dinner. I should
have seen it then, but I was so wrapped up
in this man that I lost myself in him. I took
every excuse he gave to me.

When I should have questioned everything
that he did. But I thought that he loved me
as I did him. Uugh, this is so frustrating!
So dayum confusing, still even though it's
been over a year now. I still can't wrap my
head around it, even when I play it back in
my head.

*2019: Lisette and Mary were at the
restaurant when I came in to meet
them there. It was lady's night and we
were out just to have fun and kick it
for a minute. Because I had called
Rashid before I went into the
restaurant just to see where he was
and to also know if we were still on
for tonight. But he did not pick up the
phone, which he is constantly always
on. That phone is always glued to his
ear or that he's receiving text messages
from someone.*

When he didn't answer, and Mary Jane called me and said let's go out and eat or whatever; I just said okay. Before I had went in the spot.

I checked my phone one last time thinking that maybe he had called or something and I didn't hear the phone ring. But nothing, not a dayum thing. Not even a fucckn text telling me that he was going to be tied up or something.

When I went in, there was Mary Jane and she was with Lisette and they were laughing a little bit so I went over and started kickn it with them and shyt. You know how we girls do when we get away from our men. We talk, not necessarily about men, but about other things. But I cannot lie to you, sometimes it's mostly about men, I can't fake that shyt...And while I was kickn it with them, I kept an eye on my phone for just in case. And Lisette peeped that shyt.

'Ma, please put that fuckn phone down and enjoy yourself. Whoeva that nicca is, I'm sure that he can wait.

I mean, if his dyck is that hard up, he can get some grease or something and jack off in the bathroom until you get there, shyt!' 'Lisette!!' Monique said in shock.

'I'm just being honest Ma, fo real tho...'

'Oh, my Lawd Jesus, help us and our wicked ways...' Both Mo and Lisette lol

'Baby, you know that you looks at Mary Jane like don't even try it.

'Aw, come off that shyt Mary Jane, you know that you get some dyck to. I know that man of yours be wearn that coochie out ! Lisette and Mo just die laughing giving each other High Fives. Mary Jane just looks at the both of them and does a shy giggle…

'I'm not one to brag, but he does wear it out when he gets it going...' All three just bust out laughing.

'See gurl, I know that he does, you need to stop hiding behind that Bible and just keep it real...'

'Mo, I do keep it real...'Yeah, right, sure you do.

Just that you be trippn with all of that Bible thumpn shyt that you be doin.' Mo said laughing.

'Well Mo, we all need Jesus...'

*'The only tyme that I need Jesus is when I call his name in the bedroom...*they all just die laughing. And then they noticed that their getting a lot of attention from the customers from their loud behavior.

But what little did I know that Rashid was with that skank ass bitch ho Katrina Middleton. Laying up with her nasty ass. have a phat ass?' Rashid, wha da fuc...'Nah Kat, I mean that in a good way.'
As Katrina rolls over on her back and looks at him.

'Well you betta mean that shyt in a good way, or else I am gettn my phat ass as you call it da fuck outta here...'
'Nah Baby, don't be like that, I was just sayn that you have a nice ass is all.

I especially love it when I'm hittn it from behind and seein that shyt jiggle...'

*'Shid, you so stupooid.' As she said with
a smile on her face. She then sits up and
leans towards him grabbing his dick and
says 'So Baby, you wanna hit it from da
back again and watch what my ass do
now?'*

*'Oh, hell yeah, now you're talking that
shyt that I wanna hear...'*

*'Ma, will you please put that
fucckn phone back in your
pocketbook, dayum you see dat
nicca ain't even thinkn about you.'*
Lisette says in disgust as the lady's are
now standing outside of the restaurant.

*'He could be tied up in a business
meeting or something?'*

*'Ma, really? It's 10 fucckn thirty at
night, what type of business meeting
that is going on at this tyme of night? I
mean really, come on now!'*

*She's right Mo, I don't think that there
is any type of business going on this
tyme of night unless it's some monkey
business.*

When Mary Jane said that, that hit a nerve with Monique, because even though she claims to be Holier than now Christian, she does have a point. No business executive conducts business this late at night. After hearing that Mo puts her phone back in her pocketbook and hugs Mary and Lisette and says good night to them both and they all went their separate ways. With Monique still wondering where the hell is Rashid?

By the time that Mo reaches her car, her phone rings, she quickly reaches for it and sees that it's Rashid, she answers.

'Hello Baby, I've been so worried about you, I've been calln and calln and all that its been doing is going straight to your voice mail. Is everything okay?'

'Hey Baby, yeah, yeah, everything is all gud here.

Sorry that your calls been going to voice mail. You know how it is when you're puttin up wires and shyt, sometimes it may block out the calls or some shyt like that...' He said whispering.

'Yeah, I understand Baby, I'm just glad that you're okay.'

'Mo, I'm gud. Trust me...'

'Okay Baby, I love you...'

'Yeah Baby, I love you too, gotta go..'
Rashid quicky hangs up the phone before Katrina comes out of the bathroom.

Fucck, I shoulda known something was up wit dat nicca by the way that he was actn on the phone, but nooo, my dumb ass believed his punk ass. Lame dyck mutha fuccker! Putting in wiring and shyt and sometimes that blocks calls. How dumb is that shyt, and what makes it worse, I was just as dumb to believe that.

Mo is still sitting in the church, not realizing that hours have passed. And also, not realizing that same gentleman that was there earlier is back again. The nicely dress man see's Mo still sitting there in the same spot, deep in thought. Not sure if he should disturb her or not, but it is kind of late and she is in a rough area to be out by herself.

'*Uum, excuse me Miss?*' He said cautiously.

'*Huh, what??*'

'*Hi there, it's me again. I had seen you in here earlier and I noticed that you're still in here and it's very late. I hope that everything is okay?*'

'*Oh yeah, sorry, I was deep in thought, and I lost track of the tyme. What tyme is it anyway?*'

'*It's quite alright, just making sure that you were okay, because it is now 10:45pm. You've been in here almost 3 hours now.*'

'*Wow, you're right, I did lose track of the tyme, thank you so very much.*'

'*That's quite alright.*

I understand. When you're mind is troubled and you're trying to figure out what happen, what went wrong, what did you do to deserve this and I thought that I was doing everything correctly. You then start to wonder what did YOU do to end up reaching deeply into your soul and then reaching out to God with questions...'

'Humph, wow, you got all of that from me just sitting there, huh?'

'Well not exactly, I've been there and done that and it seems like that I am going through it again for some reason or another. So I know the symptoms.'
As he said with a smile on his face.

As Mo starts to get up she grabs her handbag and gather herself. *'Sorry that I kept you Pastor, you can lock up now.'*

'Oh no, I'm no pastor, I'm just a lost soul just like you are. Lost trying to find my way back again.'

'Wow, okay, well I think that I betta go on that note, because you're sayn some things that I've been sayn and prayn to God about. So, I will leave you now.'

'That's fine, do you mind if I walk you out, because showing by the car that you're driving and how you're dress, you're a perfect target for some asshole out here looking to make a score.'

'Okay, well that's not necessary, I can handle myself fairly well.'

The gentleman then smiles at Mo. *'I'm quite sure that you can. But please let me be a gentleman and escort you out to your car. It seems as though that being a gentleman these days is long gone.'*

Monique then smiles *'Okay then, you can walk me out to my car.'* The two then walks out together chatting a little bit along the way. When they reach Mo car, she unlocks the car with her remote key, for some reason she didn't want the gentleman to know about James, not just yet anyway. Mo then breaks the silence between the two... *'My name is Mo.'*

With a confused look on his face he says *'Mo, just Mo?'* With a reserve look and stance, Mo respond back by saying *'It's Monique actually'* *'Ah, that's better'*

'I like that name than just Mo.'

Mo gives a shy girl smile and say's *'And you are?'*

'John, as in John the Baptist. But in all reality, it's Johnny, God's gift.'

'It seems like your name is surrounded by God?'

'Yeah it seems like... well you drive safely home now...'

'Sure thing, God's gift...' As Mo shows him her beautiful smile.

As Johnny turns slightly away from Mo at this point, he looks at her and says *'Oh, I see that you have jokes. Well that's a good thing, because that smile suits you betta than that sad look that you had on your face earlier. Good Night Monique.'*

'Good Night Johnny.' Mo then gets in her car and drives off. Thinking about the gentleman that she just met and while she's doing that James broke her train of thought yet again... *'Mo...'*

'Uuagh, what is it, James?'

'Just wanted to point out to you that you never asked me to start the car or anything while you were with the gentleman?'

'I know James and I'm sorry for that, it was just that I don't know him, and I didn't want him thinking that I was some sort of rich bitch or anything like that.'

'Well Mo, you are driving a 2020 red Tesla Model 3. The most expensive car out there.'

'Good point James, good point.'

'And plus, I've noticed that your heart is racing like I've never seen before. 'I know James, I don't know why either James.'

'Is it because of the young gentleman that accompanied you to the car, Mo?'

Mo then looks down at the computer screen on her dashboard and yells out rather happily and embarrassed by the comment that James made *'Nooooo, not because of him!'*

'Mo?'

'Yes James?'

'Your heart is racing again...'

'Fucck you James, fucck you!!!'

72

PHASE THREE

"The Big Fight"

As Mo makes her way home from the church, her cell phones rings. She looks at the caller ID to see who it is, it's Mary Jane. She then asks James to put her on speaker phone, which he does.

'Hello Mary, what's going on, are you okay?'

'Yeah, I'm fine, just worried about you is all?'

'Yeah Girl, I'm doing okay, I'm simply fine and dandy.'

'Wow, fine and dandy, I never heard that come from you before?'

'Okay, I'm gud girl, so what's up, why are you calling me at this hour of the night?'

'We're just worried about you that's all. We've not heard from you since you left for the meeting with the investors. Lisette told me that she spoke to you last and haven't heard anything from you since about 6:30. So she called me and asked me have I heard anything from you and I became worried, so here I am.'

Mo being a bit confused, wondering what Mary meant by here I am? *'Umm Mary, exactly, where are you?*

'I'm here at your place outside of the gate with Lisette.'

'Wait, hold da fuck up, you mean to tell me that Lisette is still there waiting there for me?'

'Hmm, yeah I guess...' Mary sounding a bit confused in what's going on.

'Okay then, I'm on my way, I'll be there in five minutes' What is this girl problem?! Mo pushes the gas pedal and the Tesla whips through traffic with ease.

'James?'

'Yes Mo?'

'Open the gate, just the gate and let them in, but not the house.'

'Very well then, it's opening now.'

'Thank you, James.' 'Quite welcome Mo.'

By this time, Mo whips around the corner as she enters her place she then drives up and parks the car outside of the garage where Lisette and Mary is waiting for her. When Mo gets out of her car, Mary rushes towards Mo and gives her a hug.

'Oh girl, am so glad that you're okay, I became so worried about you!'

'Girl, I'm fine, I'm perfectly fine thank you, am sorry that you had to come way out here for nothing. She stares at Lisette.

'Girl it's no problem, I was just scared that something had happened to you.' *'Well thank you for coming out here and staying with Lisette.'* All three then walks towards the house and Mo asked James to open the door. Lisette then mumbles under her breath saying *'Need to get your ass a man instead of talking with that fucckn computer...'*

Mo turns and looks at Lisette and then turn back continuing to walk into the house waving her hand as to say no, not now Lisette, now is not the time.

As they enter Mos' home they go over and sit down and wait to see what Mo has to say about her disappearance.

'*Well....*' Lisette says in a disrespectful tone.

'*Well what?*'

'*Where the hell have you been all this tyme?*'

'*That's none of your business first off. I'm a grown ass woman, so I can be anywhere that I wanna be, without answering to no one. THANK YOU!*' Mo said with a stern voice.

'*Come on you guys, knock it off. After all of the hell that we've been through together, there is no need for this.*'

'*It's not me Mary, it's her, and she's the one who is being all evasive and everything.*'

Mo then looks at Lisette... '*Oh, so it's on me now, really?*'

'Yeah Ma, it is. Ever since last year when all of da shyt hit the fan, you've been distance, explosive at work, going off on everyone...so yeah, it's all on you.'

'Okay then, I'll take the blame for everything that went on back then, but hell, you're in this shyt too, so you're not smellin all clean either.'

'Really Mom, I mean really Mom? You think that I'm at fault!'

'Hell yeah! if you want to keep this shyt real. Let's keep it real then. You knew that I was messing around with Rashid, you end up fuckn him too. Really Lisette!'

'Okay Mom, yeah I knew, and I am so very sorry for that. I didn't mean for it to get that far, I shoulda broke it off with dat limp dyck bastard long before it got to that point. 'Guys, guys, please come on, there's no need for this, really. What happened back then, it happened. We all got into trouble.'

'Really Mary, really? All that you did was beat da hell out of the bastard truck.' And then Mary turned and looked at Mo not believing in what she had said.

'Well Mo, I did it all for you and Lisette. He hurt you both, so he had to get pay back some sort of way.'

'Yeah I know, so we all came out of that burned by him.' Mo said.

'We almost went to jail ova that fuckn shyt.'

'Yeah, we sure did...' Mo said as she places her hand down on the counter top in the kitchen. ***'We almost surely did'*** Mo head is hanging low in disgust.

Mary then stood up and said ***'Listen guys, we've been hurt by this guy so let's let it go, there is no need for us to continue to let him come between us now.'*** Mo and Lisette both agreed.

'Ma listen, I know what he did to us was wrong, especially me, I was wrong, please forgive me for doing that to you...to us. Look in the end, we all almost went to jail ova that nicca.'

'I know Lise, I know, remember I was there as well. We both been through hell because of him. And I am too sorry.' After hearing and saying that, Lisette and Mo come together and embrace each other tightly. Mary is there watching all of this take place.

'Aw that's so sweet. I think that we all should say a prayer...' Lisette and Mo both yells

'NO!' at the same time. Mary stands there in shock, Lisette and Mo both laughs and grabs Mary by the arm and brings her in for a group hug. Girls for life.

'Okay, okay, now I need for you guys to get the fucck outta here so that I can get some sleep,

I've been up since 2:30 am. So, my black ass is tired as a mutha fuccker...'

Both Lisette and Mary both smile and say Okay and they both grab their things and leave. Mo starts walking towards her bedroom.

'James.'

'Yes Mo?'

'Lock up the House will you please.'

'Consider it done Mo.'

'You're the best James.'

'I know Mo, I know...'

Mo then takes off her clothes and hangs them up and she goes and gets in the shower that James already has prepared for her. Now her naked frame is in the steamy hot shower, thinking yet again about the events that occurred in 2019. And she says to herself, ***No, no. I am not going to do this to myself, not this time. Tonight I'm going to get some sleep.***

She then steps out of the shower and dries herself off and goes and gets in bed. She lies down and closes her eyes, and suddenly, she is fast asleep. She fell asleep so fast, that she didn't even bother to tell James at what time to wake her up. No dreams of her past, no nothing. Just nice peaceful sleep.

Next thing she knows, Mo hears her phone ringing, she jumps up outta bed and yells.

'James!'

'Yes Mo, I'm right here.'

'What tyme is it!!

'It's exactly 9 A.M.'

'Oh shyt, I'm late, I'm so fucckn late...why didn't you wake me up damnit James!

'Well for one Mo, you didn't assign me to Mo, so how could I wake you up?'

'Assign my ass James,
you know that I'm
supposed to be at the
station by now...damnit!

Now get the shower
going!'

'But Mo, can I interject something here, if I may?'

'What da fucck is it James and make it quick!'

'How can a boss be late when you own the company?' After hearing that, Mo pauses for a minute and she thought about what James said and she came to realization that James was right. I am the boss now, with Five Hundred Million Dollars in my bank account in which no one knows about and more to come, how can a boss be late?

'Well, I just be dayum James. You absolutely right, I am the boss. But still, I gotta stay on point here James, I can't be slippn, that's how businesses fail, once they get on that level, they fall off. And I don't wanna do that. So, call the station and tell the staff that I'll be there around 11 and we're having a staff meeting. You got that James?'

'Yes Mo, I did, I'm calling the station now and informing them that there will be a staff meeting at 11 A.M. Should I start the coffee as well, Mo?

'Duhhh, yes James, please start the coffee.'

After Mo gets out of the shower, she quickly puts on her makeup and she chooses one of Versace's design dresses and sends a pair of Jimmy Choo's flats to the front. She rushes into the kitchen and grabs the cup of coffee that James made then she goes to the foyer and puts on the flats.

'Mo?'

'Yes James, what is it?' Sounding frustrated.

'What car shall I start?'

'Aww shyt, I left the Tesla out didn't I!

'Yes Mo, you did.'

'What's the weather going to be like today?

'No rain in the forecast, just partly cloudy with the highs being in 80's.'

'Okay, well that's good, so nothing won't happened to my baby then, okay so go and start up the Range Rover, the white one.'

'Very good choice Mo, I'll meet you in the Rover.'

Mo then stands up and looks in the mirror and says, *'Oh well even during a rush job, your ass still looks good.'* As she grabs her Versace's handbag and rushes out the door to the 2020 white Range Rover.

She opens the door and puts the handbag in the passenger seat and places the coffee cup in the cup holder and then she climbs in and peels off heading down her driveway and then onto I-95 to get to the radio station. She then turns on the radio to listen to the station to hear what is being said on Air. She hears Dalvin on the air. *'Aiight, Aiight, what's up my peeps.*

This is ya Man, Dee Goode, comn at'cha with some real love fo ya. As you very well know that we had some very, very, important people here at the station yesterday talkn about how we can curb the violence between Blacks and police officers here in Philly. And it was a very gud show, we had our Leading Lady, Monique, Leaders from BLM movement, people from the City Council Board. The Mayor and we even had the Governor on da phone. So that was an awesome meeting yesterday.'

'Yeah Dee Goode, our Queen Mo, she carried herself like a true Queen that she is. I mean when she spoke, everyone listened. That just shows us in how well respected that our First Lady Mo, is in the community. Dats real love right there.' Jaylen says standing in for Mo since she was late.

Mo continues to listen to the show as she blushes about what is being said about her.

'Those are my real nicca's right there. Dem dudes has been down wit me fo real since day one. Even when that Bitch Nic...nooo Mo, slow ya roll gurl, let's not go there, not today ass, not right now.' As she races down 95. She was listening so hard that she almost missed her exit, she quickly turns and wheeled down the ramp and pushes on the brakes as she almost runs into a car waiting at the red light at the bottom of the ramp.

'Slow down girl, slow da fuck down.' As she finally calms her nerves she starts to drive more carefully now and she makes the right turn down the street from the station. And there standing outside of the booth, there he was, standing there looking worried until he sees the white Range Rover heading in that direction, and here comes that smile on his face.

Buddy. Mo then slows down as she pulls into the driveway that leads to her parking spot, no matter how late that she is, she just has to speak to her old friend Buddy.

'Hey there Buddy, how you doing?'

'I'm doing good Mo, I was worried about you, you wasn't here at your normal tyme.'

'Yeah, I know Buddy, am sorry. I overslept and well, you know how it is...' As she gives him one of her smiles that he just can't be angry at.

'Yeah I know how it is, and that's all dat it betta be, betta not be no other mutha fuccker layn in my place beside you...'

Mo with a surprised look on her face couldn't believe what Buddy said, and he seems like he was pretty dayum serious too.

'Buddddyyy, come on now, you know that no one is gonna hit this ass accept you.'

'Aiight, betta not have no other nicca layn up in my spot...'

'Buddy, are you jealous?'

'Dayum Skippy...' Mo then laughs and reaches out and grabs Buddy's hand

. She then strokes the back of his hand with her thumb to help calm the old man down…

'Come Buddy, lemme see that beautiful smile of yours, come on now.'

And then just that quick, Buddy flashes that smile of his... *'Ooo, there it is. I see it now'* As Mo starts laughing.

'Go on gurl, get your ass to your spot before you give this old man a heart attack...' as he laughs with Mo. As Buddy raises the security arm Mo drives right in and finds her spot gets out of the car with her handbag and coffee. And there at the door was Mary Jane.

'Gurl, you're late...'

'I know Mary, I know...'

'The investors are going to be pissed, you know how those white men are, they don't like it when you start messing wit their money.'

'Gurl, I got this, not worried about them ever again.

' As Mo rushes pass her and heads towards her office.

'James, are you with me?'

'Yes Mo, always.'

'Okay, unlock the door.'

'Consider it done.'

'Okay James, great.' By the time that Mo reaches her door to her office, she pushes it open and goes over to her desk and plops everything down on her desk and she flops down in her chair.

'Okay James, what tyme is it?'

'It is exactly 10:55.'

'Okay thanks James, call the crew, all of them. And notify the guys in the studio.'

'Consider it done Mo.'

James then comes on the intercom and announces that Mo wants to have a meeting with everyone in the station. And in the studio, a red-light flashes, to tell the guys in the studio that there is a meeting getting ready to take place

. So, they then put the music on for continuous play back. They take off their headsets and heads towards Mo's office. Because they dare not be late, or they will get hit with a $1,000.00 fine.

Once everyone arrives, Mo sits there with a smile on her face and she starts to speak as she gets up from behind her desk.

'Good Morning everyone, sorry that I'm late, I overslept, so please forgive me.

However, I do have some exciting news to tell you.'

Now she has everyone attention. But no one was really concerned about her being late, they understood that Mo is a successful businesswoman, and they know that she wouldn't be late without a good reason. Now everyone is listening to what she has to say.

'But first and foremost, I want to thank each and every one of you for hanging in there with me. Especially during those hard times last year. So, I really do appreciate that. And thank you.' Everyone starts to murmur amongst themselves, all showing their smiles in appreciation.

'Now then for the big news. 100 HOT FM is officially mines. I own every crack, every stone, every piece of equipment in this building.' A huge hush fell over the staff and crew with shock and amazement over their faces.

Jaylen spoke first… 'Are you serious right now Mo?' Mo then looks at Jaylen with a wide smile on her face and she said it again. 'Jaylen, yes I am. As of yesterday at 6am, I bought 100 HOT FM.

'What about the investors Mo?' Dalvin asked.

'Them greedy white fuuckers didn't see me comn. When I told them, what happen and how it happened, they couldn't say shyt, I left them fuuckers speechless.'

91

The staff and the rest of the crew just gave a huge cheer. They couldn't be happier for her, because they all know what happened a year ago.

'Okay, okay now listen. Regardless if I own this or not, we cannot get caught napping, you hear me. I want you all to stay on top of your game. No matter how much I love y'all, I will fi'ya your asses with the quickness. Do you understand me?' Mo says with a stern voice. Everyone yells out, *'Yeah Mo, we got you, we got you!'*

'Good, now get your asses back to work. James is recording all of this to relay it back to the night shift crew. Okay, so y'all make me proud and go and earn me some more money. They all start talking as they leave Mo's office. Mary remains behind.

'Is this the reason in why you were late getting home last night, you were out celebrating, wasn't you?'

'No Mary, I just had a lot of shyt on my mind yesterday after the meeting and then that shyt with Lisette. So I just drove around Philly and ended up at some church and I just got out and went inside and just talked to God.'

'Wow, you went into a church, now that's news.' Mary said smiling.

'Don't even go there Mary. I just had a lot of weight on me and I just had to release it.'

'Did you?'

'Did I what?'

'Release it?'

'No Mary, I didn't.' Mo then eases back into her chair and went into deep thought. Mary sees that Mo is off someplace else, so she makes her exit. Leaving Mo there in thought. When Mo realizes that she's alone. *'James?'*

'Yes Mo?'

'Do you think that you can find that church again?'

'Yes Mo.'

'Okay then, put it in the GPS.'

'Consider it done Mo.'

'Thank you, James.'

'You're quite welcome Mo.

' *'Mo?'*

'Yes James?'

'Are you going back to see him?' Mo said in confusion.

'Who, who are you talking about James?'

'The young man that you met last night, I think that his name is Johnny?'

Looking shocked and confused, *'Johnny, no. I'm going to find peace within myself*

James, if you must know.' Mo said with sarcasm in her voice.

'Mo?'

'Yes, what is it now James???'

'Your heart is racing again.'

'You know what James, fucck you!'

'Yes of course Mo.'

Mo then grabs her handbag and keys and heads out of the office, telling James to make sure that the office is secure. She then heads for the Rover which is already started by James, she backs up and started heading towards the security booth where Buddy is there. She slows down and rolls down the window.

'I heard the great news Mo, I couldn't be more prouder of you. When I heard the news, I said to myself, that's my girl. Sho dem crackers who they're fucckin wit.'

'Aww, thank you Buddy. That means a lot to me. So, thank you.'

'My pleasure Baby. Now you are gonna keep ole Buddy on as security, aren't you?'

Buddy looking at her with concerns.

'Buddy, there is no way in hell would I eva get rid of you. You're my heart...' Hearing her say that, Buddy almost shed a tear...

'Go on Gurl, git outta here before you make me cry up here.' As Buddy raises the arm so that Mo can leave. Mo then pulls out and looks down at her GPS to see which direction that she needs to go in order to find that church that she was at last night.

She follows the directions exactly. And there it is, the church that she was at last night. It looks much different than how it was looking last night.

Mo pulls into a parking spot now that she can see where to park at. She then gets out of the Rover and looks around before entering the Church, the church is old, it seems to be falling apart in some places. As she looks on, she can't believe that she was even there last night. She then opens the door of the church, the door creaked while opening. The sunlight changes everything, the pews look all beat up, some were missing. Trash thrown everywhere and there were broken windows. Mo was in complete shock seeing how beat to hell the church looked.

She continues walking inside to where she thought that she was sitting at last night. She brushes off the dust from the seat of the pew and sat down. And looked up at the podium and sees a broken figure of Jesus hanging there on the cross. Mo says to herself

'Humph, just like me, broken.'

Mo then goes back into deep thought again, about 2019 and all that happened. Rashid sleeping with Katrina and Lisette, while being married to Ne'a. Who was fucking Dalvin. Who knew???

As Mo was in deep thought, the young man from last night had entered the church as well. And he sits down in one of the back pews and start thinking about his past Both seems to be wrestling with their own battles, conflicts, pain, broken heart, the scars that life has given them trying to pick up the pieces again which is hard to do, so hard, because now, at this moment, it's so hard to trust anyone. Because everyone seems to be about game now, or that they say that they love you when after the honeymoon is over, you still find yourself alone, even when you're with them or not.

Both Mo and Johnny seemed to be in a battle within themselves, that they both are sitting there with their hands over their faces, trying to make sense of this thing called Life…

Then a voice broke both of their thoughts… *'Mo, he's here…'* Mo opens her eyes from her deep thought in bewilderment she looks at her arm and shh, James. *'Who's here, James?'*

As Mo is trying to whisper while trying to look around to see who James is talking about. And Johnny is sitting there looking all around as well, trying to figure out where is that man's voice coming from that he heard.

He's looking under the pews, looking up above him, thinking that it maybe God speaking to him or something. So, then he looks and spots Mo, her head is moving as she is speaking to James.

'It's that young fellow from last night, Johnny.' Not realizing that now, Johnny has gotten up and started walking to where Mo is sitting. *What, where..?*

'Well I don't consider myself a young fellow, but tell whoever that is that you're speaking with Thank you. He says with a smile on his face.

Mo then puts her other hand on top of her wrist, thinking that may stop James from speaking. Being rather embarrassed, She gets up and grabs her handbag... *'Oh my, I'm sorry, I thought that I was in here by myself. I hope that I didn't disturb you.'* As Mo is moving her hands around nervously hoping that she doesn't forget anything as she is trying to make her escape.

'Oh no, you didn't disturb me. It was whoever said that he's here and that young fellow. That's who disturb me. Because I already know that I'm disturb.' He said flashing his smile.

Mo faintly laughs as she is trying hard to make her exit. *'Oh, yeah, that's James.'*

Johnny then looked puzzled, because he doesn't see anyone else there, just her. *'Umm, James. Who is James?'*

'He's my...' And before Mo could say another word, she thought about it in that spilt second, if I tell him who James is, either he would think that I'm totally loony or something. I must not tell him who James is.

'He's no one...' Mo said quickly. *'No one, huh? Well that no one sure does know my name. So please tell me Monique, how can no one know my name?'* Mo couldn't answer that, so she had to change the conversation rather quickly, before this gets even more awkward.

'So, what are you doing here? Do you stay here or something?' As she said, looking all awkward, hoping that he wouldn't ask any more questions about who is James?

'Well no Monique, I don't stay here. I come here from time to time and just sit back to think and pray. And now to look at how much that this church has fallen apart ova the years. It's simply shocking to me.

This church was something else back in its hay day'

'Oh, so you use to go here?'

'Yes, I did, quite some time ago.' As he said while he's looking up and down at the church being disgusted on how the church looks now and how he had remembered it.

'And Oh, as we continue with this conversation, I haven't forgotten about the elephant in the room.'

'What elephant in the room, what on earth are you talking about?' Sounding confused.

'Who is James ...'

'Dayum!' Mo says under her breath. It seems like he won't let that shyt go.

Damnit James, you and your bad timing.

'Mo?' After hearing that, Johnny starts to look at Mo and her handbag.

'Hmm, it seems like to me, that voice that I keep hearing is coming from your handbag.'

'Who, what is, what are you talking about?' She said nervously.

'That voice that I heard earlier. The one that you call James?'

'Mo?'

'Shyt James, would you please shut up.' Mo is saying to herself as she is trying to turn the volume down and cut him off. But she is having a difficult time in doing it, James continues.

'Mo?'

Johnny then smile, watching Mo struggles, it amuses him. So, he takes one of his arms and puts it across his chest and takes his hand and covers his mouth, trying to keep from laughing at Mo as she continues to struggle to turn James off.

'Mo?'

Johnny can't take it no more, because he's cracking up…

'Monique, I think that you should answer that guy or else he's never gonna shut up.' Johnny said because he is dying laughing at this time.

'Shyt!' She says being exhausted from trying to hide James.

'What is it James?'

'Just wanted to inform you that your heart is racing again.' Now Mo is totally embarrassed. She just doesn't know what to do or how to respond to that.'

'Aw dayum James, I know, I know.'

Johnny is still laughing so as he is trying to regain his composer,

'Okay Monique, do you mind now telling me who this James is and how does he know my name?'

'Dayum, aiight, he's my personal assistant and how he knows your name, he heard us talking last night and he heard you tell me your name.

There, are you happy now?' Mo then falls back against one of the pews she is completely embarrass now.

'Wait, he's your personal assistant and he heard me tell you my name. And he remembers that?

'Yes he does, he remembers everything, he's almost real, he can become annoying at times, but yeah, he does. He helps me out a lot.'

'Wow, that's amazing. This technology thing is amazing now. They have everything.'

He said shaking his head.

'Yeah, it has. Now, getting back to the other question that I asked you, since I did answer yours.'

'What question is that Monique?'

'That you use to go here, but I did ask you did you stay here?'

'Well Monique, I did answer your questions, I don't stay here, I just come here and think about all the things that went wrong in my life. All of the pain that I've gone through, heartache, all of the scars that love has left me with.'

'Humph, man, I can tell you about love, pain, and heart break. You're singing to the choir.' Johnny stands there with a surprising look on his face.

'I just bet you can, Monique, I just bet you can.'

'Johnny, you have no idea of what pain is or what heartbreak is, trust me. You could write a book about my life and what I've gone through.'

'Well then Monique, why don't you tell me what you've gone through?'

'Nah, I'll take a rain check on that one Johnny.' Then Mo just thought about it for moment and just said *'You know what Johnny, fucck it.'* Mo then just flops down hard on one of the pews that was behind her. She is just exhausted; she just needs to get this monkey off her back.

'You know Johnny, you men ain't shyt.' Johnny then pulls up a broken dirty chair that was laying there on the floor opens it up and sits down and crosses his legs and starts to listen to Mo talk.

'Some of you men ain't shyt.' Mo then looks at Johnny, waiting on a response from him. He just sits there looking her. With no expression.

'What, you're not going to say anything, you're just going to sit there?'

'Um, yeah. I mean, I'm waiting for you to say something that's not surprising to me. Not something that I don't already know.'

Surprised by his remark. Mo continues... *'Yeah, some of you men ain't shyt. You come into a female life and destroy them. We give and give, you fuckin assholes just take and take.'* Again, she looks at Johnny. And again Johnny continues to just sit there looking at her.

'You know what Johnny, just forget it. You just don't get it.'

'Huh, what? What did I do?' Johnny says with a surprise look on his face.

'I mean all that you're doing is just sitting there and not saying anything. So, I quit, I give up. You men just don't get it or just don't want to get it.'

'Monique, listen. I get what you're saying, that we men ain't shyt. I get that part. Well some of us men ain't shyt. But what you fail to understand, that some of us men do care, we do get it, we do understand that you women do get hurt in the process and most importantly, we do listen. That's how you build a relationship with that someone. You listen to them, you hear their words. You feel

their pain. A new man that's coming into someone's life, they have to understand that the man that was there before you, they have hurt them deeply. So now, you have to pick up the broken pieces.

With hopes that they can love again, if not with you, maybe with someone else. Because if it's not with you, at least what you can get out of it, is a true friend.

So yes Mo, I do get it. Please go on. Because one thing for sure, I do listen. I just don't give any type of opinions or advice. Because opinions are just like assholes, everyone got one. You feel me?'

With a surprise look on her face, she responds back'*Yeah Johnny, I feel you. Well anyway, I fell madly in love with my ex- business partner, who at the time, I didn't know was married. So not only was I his side piece, he had another side piece as well. And then come to find out, his wife had a side piece too.*

Johnny then sits up and says, '*Woah, wait a minute, you mean to tell me that the dude that you were involved with, he was married, am I assuming that correctly. And his wife was screwing someone else to?*'

'*Yep, you got it.*'

'*Dayum.*'

'*Oh no. just wait, that's only the half of it.*'

'*What, there is more?*'

'*Yes, it is, not only was my so called lame dyck lover screwing over me and his wife, he was also fuccking my daughter...*' When Johnny heard that, he just could not believe his ears.

'*Wow.*'

Yeah. We went into business together (sniff) by starting a local radio station. And we did, but by him being such a handsome tall light-skinned man, I just fell for him, hook line and sinker. I mean this man totally had my heart. That's why I say that you men just don't get it. You come into a woman's life, we give you our heart, we give you our body and soul completely and what do you with it, you take it and dog us out. And all you do is leave broken pieces behind.

*You men ain't shyt. That's why it's so hard for me to trust anything that a man has to say to me, because all of it is a bunch of shyt..*Johnny continues just to sit there and listen.

But now, Monique is looking at him in the light, this Johnny dude, he isn't a bad looking guy. Nice suit can't really tell who made it, but you can tell that it's tailored made, and oh wow, red bottom shoes, now I know that cost a pretty penny right there. And before she realizes it, her heart begins to race again and that would mean...

'Mo?'

'Not now James.'

Okay.' Johnny laughs. *'Does he always do that (sniff)?'*

'Yeah, he does, his timing is especially bad today.' Johnny laughs again. *'Okay, I'll take your word for it. So, you were saying that you two went into business together and started a radio station?'*

'Oh yeah, we did. And we got some people who is my ride or die people, we got them from the neighborhood, Dalvin, who cannot stand Rashid, as a matter of fact, Rashid and Dalvin and Jaylen got into a hard hitting fight about this?' Now Johnny is looking a bit confused.

'Jaylen, who is this Jaylen?'

'Oh, Jaylen is a Music producer and song writer and sometimes he helps me out at the station. Rumor has it that he has a secret crush on me, but I dunno, all that I know is that Dalvin beat the living shyt outta Rashid.'

'And Dalvin, does he have a crush on you too?'

'Huh, I don't think so, he's young, and a playa as well. But he has my back, always. And then there's this skank ass Katrina...' and Johnny interrupts again... *'and Katrina is who?'*

'Dayum, my bad Johnny, I keep talking to you like you know these people. Dalvin Goode is the DJ that I have at the station, and Jaylen Reed is like I said, he's a music producer and song writer. And Katrina Middleton, this skank ass Ho, now she's a real piece of work right there.'

'I take it that you don't like her very much, do you?' And the look that Mo gave Johnny, like the saying goes, if looks could kill, Johnny would be six feet under right about now.

'Johnny man, please, I can't stand that bitch. Whew! Okay, anyway, then there's Ne'a Temple, that was Rashid wife, that I didn't know about at the time. He kept or tried to keep all of that a secret from me, so I didn't know. He just basically lied to me, just so that I could be another notch on that so call dyck of a gun. Worthless piece of shyt. Humph!

' As Monique raises her hand to the Heavens shaking her head.

Johnny continues to sit there watching Monique go through all of these emotions, wanting to help, wanting to offer some sort of comfort. But he knows from experience that a person has to get all of that out of their system before they can be able to heal properly.

Mo continues on and then.

'There is Mary Jane Norton, she has a heart of gold. She's

a self-proclaimed Christian and Bible thumper.

'Why do you say that she's a self-proclaimed Bible thumper?'

Mo starts to laugh. *'Cause she always getting the verses in the Bible wrong, but she's good peeps though. Love her.'*

'Did she sleep with Rashid too?'

'Oh hell no, she's married. Humph, which doesn't mean anything. But nah, she didn't sleep with him. Surprisingly enough, that's the one person who that nicca didn't sleep with, now that I think about it.

Humph. Anyway Johnny, yeah, found out that Rashid was sleeping with Katrina and sometimes he would have her at his place when his wife would be at work.'

'And that's Ne'a, right?'

'Yeah, Ne'a. She was working all these crazy ass hours and no one was the wiser that she was actually smashing Dalvin. Which Dalvin didn't care, because he couldn't stand Rashid. And he knew that Rashid and me had this thing going on. So, anything that Dalvin could do to get back at Rashid, he did. So, bangin' his wife was no biggie.' Johnny is just sitting there listening intently. Not saying hardly anything, he's just listening.

'Wow.' That's basically all that Johnny could say at this point. By this time, Mo has gotten up out of the pew and started expressing herself physically with her body antics.

'Hey Yo Johnny man, this nicca was straight up trippin, Yo!' Johnny was just sitting there witnessing all of her emotions coming out.

She went from being, bouncing all over the place. To where now the pain is starting to set in.

Which is the norm when it comes to pain like this. When someone hurts you, it cuts you deep. It's more than just a cut, it's just so hard to explain it. When they say that love hurts, they ain't joking, because it does.

As Johnny continues to sit there watching Monique, he looked into her eyes. He could see that the pain is still there, even after a whole year that has gone by, the hurt and pain is still there. The sadness in her beautiful soft light brown eyes is still there. The hurt and pain of what Rashid did to her is still there, the burning hatred that is on the inside of her is boiling like a pot on a stove. Johnny couldn't do or say anything to comfort her, he just had to let her get it all out of her system.

'Johnny man, you men ain't shyt. And don't even have me talk about my ex-husband, you don't want me to go there. Nah Bruh, you really don't want me to go there.

' Mo then lowers her head, tears started falling from her eyes. The guilt of all of the lies that men has ever told this young woman is coming out.

 All of the love that she ever gave to a man and he returned it by either lying to her or cheating on her is coming out.

'Monique, if I may say something? I mean I know that I had told you that I wasn't going to say anything, however, I feel that I have to at this point.'

Monique scuffles in the pew (sniff, sniff) *'Aww man, go ahead, fucck. I've heard it all...so there's nothing that you can say that can't make it any worst than what it is right now.'* With tears still falling from her eyes.

'I'm sorry.'

When Johnny said that to her, she just let the tears flow then. Because for some reason or another, she believed him.'

'Fuuuuuccccckkkkk, why you go and say that for, dayum you!!' Monique continues to cry. Something that she hasn't done in a very long time.

'Fucck you Johnny.' As she tries to crack a smile through her pain. As Monique tries to gather herself, she goes on telling Johnny, this complete stranger in what happened a year ago.

'Johnny man, that nicca Rashid would call me after he's been with that skank ass Ho Katrina and then tries to lay up with me and with me none the fucckn wiser. How fucckn dumb was that shyt, huh?!

THE BEGINNING

'One-night Ne'a slipped up and came home early and Rashid was there. She didn't expect for him to be there because the nicca is always gone. So Ne'a came steppn in the crib with the smell of a mans cologne and walked by Rashid. And Rashid caught wind of that smell because he had smelled it earlier when he was at the gym.

My nicca Dalvin had on that same cologne, Versace or some shyt. So when Ne'a walked by, Rashid caught the smell and he called her out on it. Sayn some shyt, who's cologne you got on. So, the nicca went straight buggn.

Ne'a finally had enough and called his punk ass out (by this time Monique is sitting back against the pew making hand motions, trying to get her point across).

And see, here's the thing, I had finally had enough of his shyt to. Because every time that we were together, his phone would always go off. And when I'd questioned him about it, he would always say that it's business. So, I had asked him to let me see his phone. The nicca ducked and dodged and kept telln me that he's not gonna let me see his phone. So,

I wanted to prove to him that I really and truly loved him. So, I tossed him my phone to let him go through it. And I told him, now that's trust. So, let me see your fucckn phone. And again, he said no. So, what I did was, I had one of my girls call him from an unlisted number or blocked number. I forgot how I set that shyt up, but I put that mutha fucker on blast and he failed badly.

Check out what he did though, when my girl called him, this asshole got up and went into the bathroom and came back out later, sayn that he had to go. I knew from that point on, that fuccker was cheatn on me.'

(Johnny then interrupts) 'So, what happened with him and his wife?'

'Oh yeah, she already knew that he was fucckn other bitches, she called him out on it to. And if that fuccker couldn't dance, he sure did that day. Because he dip and dodge all of that shyt. And she finally told him that she was fucckn Dalvin, and that nicca was pissed, do you hear me! Boi was that nicca pissed.

Now listen to this, Katrina tried to play him to, this is how dumb the nicca was, she told him that she was pregnant and that he was the father, that nicca ate that shyt up. He believed her and she didn't tell him no different. She just wanted to keep him in check.'

117

'Boi, that's something.'

'No Johnny, wait, that's only just the tip of this iceberg.' Johnny then eased back in the chair.

Rashid world as he knew it, was starting to come crumbling down. So, by Ne'a putting him on blast and finding out that she was screwn Dalvin. And then Katrina telln his dumb ass that she was pregnant, don't even compare to what my ride or die chic Mary Jane did to him.'

'Whoa, wait, I thought that she was a Christian?'

'Mary can be gangsta when she wants to be. That's my girl right there.'

'Uumm, Okay.' Was all that Johnny could say. *Yeah, anyway, that was nothing compared to what me, my daughter (then Johnny looks at her strangely). Yeah, some how, my daughter got mixed up in this shyt to. Because she opened a fake Facebook account and trolled through Facebook and found him on there, so that's how we found out that he had a wife.*

When my home girl found out what he did to me we all started planning on how to get that

mutha fuccker back. We came up with a plan that we will destroy his pride and joy. His whip!

We then had to really plan this shyt out, because once we did that, he may figure out that we may have had something to do with it. As a result, we came up with an alibi. We came up with a plan of getting some movie tickets in or around the time that we planned on trashing his whip. I wanted to torch his shyt, but Mary Jane and Lisette didn't want to go Waitin' To Exhale on his punk ass. Therefore, we ended up smashing all of his windows, everything and got to the movies in time. So that way if the cops came sniffin round, we could tell'em that we were at the movies.'

'Did they?'

'Did they who?'

'Did the police come around?'

'Yeah, them assholes came. Detective Horatio Simmons and Burton Moats. I remember them fucckers like it was yesterday. They came around about a week or two later, asking us all kinds of questions and shyt. But our alibi was solid. But the real shyt came out when Dalvin and Rashid went at each other, when Rashid thought that he was man enough to approach him for fucckn his wife Ne'a.' And all of this shyt happened at the station, that's when all the shyt came out Dalvin proved Rashid all wrong.

119

Dalvin dusted his ass.

Door burst open, Rashid came storming into the station and goes straight at Dalvin...

Yo nicca, you fucckn my wife?' And shoves him.

Dalvin gives a funny type laugh like he's been waiting on this moment to come. *'What if I am?'*

'Yo dude, that's my fucckn wife, mutha fucc..' By this time Jaylen steps in between them. Now the whole station is out in the hallway watching all of this go down. Some in complete shock. Other's not at all surprised. The rest been waiting for this to happened.

'Mo?'

'Yes James?'

I think that you better watch the security monitor, there seems to be trouble in the outer office.' Mo quickly turns on the monitor to see what's going on outside of her office. She sees Rashid and Dalvin getting ready to go at each other and Jaylen is trying to hold them both back. And at this point in the game, Mo can care less about what happens to Rashid, she hopes that Dalvin fucck his ass up. But she has to have control, 100 HOT FM has an image to withstand.

Mo knows that something like this will not go over well with the investors. She knows that she got to make a stand. With that being said, she gets up and goes outside to try to calm things down. And in all reality, she really don't give a fucck in what happens to Rashid. When Mo comes out of her office, Rashid and Dalvin are still going at it.

'Yo mutha fuccker, you smashin my wife!'

'You know something Rah man, hell yea I'm hittin dat ass!'

'Yo Jay move man, lemme get at this mutha fuccker!'

Nah Rah, I don't think that you want no piece of this dude, fo real Yo!'

'Wait, wha…are you in on this too mutha fuccker?!' Now this is how twisted Rashid is, now that he finds out that he's not the only playa out there, he thinks now that everyone is having sex with his wife.

'Nah playa, I don't go out like that. I don't smash on married women Yo, that's your speed!'

Now Jaylen is starting to get a little pissed off at Rashid. Because now he's getting in Rashid face. Don't get it twisted, Jaylen can hold his own when he needs to. And now, he don't need to.

'What'cha sayin, huh, what'cha saying punk ass mutha fuccker, huh?

'Yo homeboy, told you, I don't go out like that. I don't mess wit other men women, that's your speed, that's what da fucck am sayin Yo!' **So now Rashid tries to flip it back on me, since I kick his ass out of my house the night before.**

'Oh that's right, that's right. You got feelings for Mo, that is right!'

Now Jaylen is somewhat surprised, because he was trying to hide his feelings from Mo, because he didn't want it to become a problem around the station. Rashid continues to call Jaylen out about his feelings towards Monique.

'Surprised that I knew about that, huh…well dumb mutha fuccker, everyone round da

station knows about your punk ass school-boy crush on Mo!'

'You know what Rah, I was trying to be a man about this whole shyt that you brought down on this station, because you've turned this whole place of business into a fucck nest. You're trying to tap every ass in this joint Yo. So, you know what, Imma let me my boi right here handle your punk ass, fo real!'

'Are you serious, this fucckin light weight. Man, I hit heavy bags bigger than his light ass!'

'Aiight then, there you go!' Jaylen steps to the side so that Dalvin and Rashid can go at each other.

'Light weight huh, I'll sho your punk ass who's a light weight!'

'Nicc....' And before Rashid could finish his sentence, Dalvin made his back dirty (in other words, Dalvin hit Rashid so hard with one punch that he floored Rashid)

Rashid checked his mouth, blood started coming out. 'Lucky shot mutha fuccker, lucky shot...'

'Well I got more for your ass, get up, get up!'

123

Rashid then made it to his feet, now their dancing around like boxers do in the ring, Rashid is talking trash trying to get inside Dalvin head. Dalvin is not having any parts of it. His main focus is finishing this fuccker up and go on bout his day.

Rashid swings and misses, Dalvin countered and hit Rashid on the left side of his jaw, which staggered Rashid, which made Rashid drop his guard, Dalvin followed up with a right cross that came out of nowhere, which finished Rashid for good.

By this time, Ne'a made her way into the station to witness all of this, watching her husband get his ass handed to him. Then she looks at Dalvin dancing around like he's Ali or something saying that he's the champ. Not only did he beat his ass he's also fucckin your wife!

Ne'a couldn't believe that Dalvin was boosting about them two having sex, especially in front of the whole radio station and the crew.

She just had to shut this down and to shut him up. '

Dalvin!' Ne'a yells. Dalvin stops dancing like he just won the heavy championship bout. He turns and looks in the direction of the yell. He see's Ne'a. And that puts a smile on his face, which quickly turns differently.

'You might have won the fight, but your dyck didn't win the battle mutha fuccker!' Ne'a then turns and leaves the radio station. During this whole time, Monique was just standing there watching this whole thing go down. Thinking that this situation is not going to go over well with the investors, she had to take a stand right then and there.

She goes over to where Rashid was trying to get up off the floor and leans down and says *'Not only are we done personally, we're done professionally as well. Now get the fucck outta my radio station, you lame dyck mutha fuccker!'* Monique stood back up and yelled out

'Someone call the trash collector; I got some trash needs to be thrown out!' Monique then turns and heads back into her office.

'It felt like a lifetime for me to get my life back together Johnny. Men have come into my life, they have lied, cheated and corrupted the word love and what it means.

125

Because what you men do, is that you get what you can and then you leave, you leave us (me) broken to where I have fix all of the pieces back together again. That's why I say that you men ain't shyt.'

Johnny just continues to sit there and watch Monique go through all of these emotions; even though it's been a year since all of this happened. To Monique, it feels like it just happened yesterday. Monique and Johnny spent hours together as Monique began telling Johnny her story, a story of love, heartbreak and pain.

'So here I am now Johnny, praying asking God for His help. Asking to help me deal with this pain that I'm dealing with. I have at times Johnny, found myself alone, praying and I continue to pray asking God to heal me from this pain. And here I am now, in this broken-down church talking to a complete stranger who I just met, telling him of my pain that I've gone through with men. And here is the fuccked up part about all of this, you are a MAN, go figure.' Monique then sits back against the pew again and she gives a slight laugh and as she wipes her eyes and wipes her running nose.

Johnny just sits there listening and then he under crosses his legs and lower his head like he has a lot on his mind. He looks like he wants to say something to Monique, maybe say something to help ease her pain. But he really didn't know what to say.

Monique notices what Johnny is doing *'What, you have nothing to say?'*

'Humph, I do have something to say Monique, but it won't help ease your pain that you're enduring right now.'

'Aw man, just go ahead and say the fucckin shyt, dayum!'

'Monique, I told you in the beginning, that's not what I do. I don't give my opinion or thoughts about anything that you tell me. Because what it seems like to me, that all that you needed is a friend.

A friend who can and will listen without any opinion or judgements. Because if a person gives an opinion, and should you follow that persons opinion and it comes out to be wrong, you then blame the person or persons who gave you their opinion and then you may lose a good friend. So, I offer no opinion. I just listen.

Surprised by his comment, Monique sees that he is a man of his word. Because he did say that he does not offer any opinion of any kind, which is unusual for anyone. Because everyone has their intake of someone else's situation.

'Johnny, I appreciate the kind gesture, but right now man, you can go ahead and say what's on your mind.' Johnny then sits back up and looks deeply into Monique eyes and he can still see the hurt that's there.

'Monique, first and foremost, I want to tell you thank you for sharing your story, even if I am a stranger (he said with a slight grin as in trying to ease some of the tension that's now there). *As I look into your eyes Monique, I can see the pain that others have caused you and it hurts me that they have hurt you. There is no excuse for that, none whatsoever. So, I am not even going to try to come up with one.*

However, like you, some of us REAL MEN, who believes in the word love, we have pretty much gone through much similar situations as you have gone through. Some much worse. '

Monique watches Johnny as he starts to explain, noticing that he's uncomfortable about talking. She sees something in him that she has seen in herself. And the way that he's talking, he's been hurt as well.

(Sniff, sniff) *'So umm, I take it that you've been hurt to?'* Johnny then pauses and looks at Monique and he gives her a faint smile.

'I have Monique, I have. But that's a story for another day, another time. Right now Monique, we're both two individuals on a quest to find our story. So right now, this is your life, this is your story. So, c'mon and let me walk you to your car.'

'Are you sure that you're not a Pastor Mr. Johnny?' Johnny gives another faint but painful smile and lowers his head as they continue to walk towards Monique's car. And Monique notices besides her car a Lexus 2020 limited edition. Monique was impressed by what she sees.

'Yes Monique, I'm sure that am not a Pastor, I'm broken, just like you.' As they reach Monique's Range Rover, Johnny stands there waiting for Monique to get inside of her car. Monique notices that and says to herself

"Dayum, and he's a gentleman too, walking me to my car, standing there making sure that nothing happens to me. That's very rare to me. You don't see that every day."

'Well, you can't be to broken Mr. Johnny...'

'Why, what do you mean Monique?'

'Is that your whip over there?' Johnny then glances at his car, gives a funny looking smile...

'Yes Monique, that is my whip as you call it. And just because a man Chariot is not broken, doesn't mean that he is...' as he said with a charming smile.

Monique opens her car door and slides in, making sure that Johnny notices her perfect body, her shapely legs, her perfect polished toes. Johnny smiles as he notices what she's doing and he closes her door.

'Very well put Mr. Johnny, very well put.'

'Have a good day Monique. And by the way, your healing has begun.'

Outro

I know that some broken women love the attention they get from being broken... But God, that ain't me... I just want to be whole again.... I just want to be loved, truly loved...by a man ... Who caresses the broken pieces of me that I already mended back together... A man who loves me for the new work of art that I am ...Can you hear me God? Just one good man... Who truly understands every aspect of how to love me, for who I am... Can you hear me??? God.

To Be Continued!

His Woman,

His Wife,

My Man

By

Monica Mason

Printed in Great Britain
by Amazon

22969925R00076